PUFFIN BOOKS
GANDHI SPEAKS

Mohandas Karamchand Gandhi (1869–1948) was a thinker, politician and leader. He shaped India's freedom movement and led the country to independence in 1947. His ideas of non-violence and Satyagraha influenced resistance movements all over the world.

Gandhi Speaks

THE MAHATMA'S WORDS FOR CHILDREN

FOREWORD BY
RAJMOHAN GANDHI

PUFFIN BOOKS

An imprint of Penguin Random House

PUFFIN BOOKS

USA | Canada | UK | Ireland | Australia
New Zealand | India | South Africa | China

Puffin Books is part of the Penguin Random House group of companies
whose addresses can be found at global.penguinrandomhouse.com

Published by Penguin Random House India Pvt. Ltd
4th Floor, Capital Tower 1, MG Road,
Gurugram 122 002, Haryana, India

Penguin
Random House
India

First published in Puffin Books by Penguin Books India 2009

ISBN 9780143330479

Typeset in Cochin by Manipal Digital Systems, Manipal

Printed at Repro India Limited

www.penguin.co.in

CONTENTS

CONTENTS

PUBLISHER'S NOTE

Mahatma Gandhi arouses many opinions among adults. But what do children think about him? Do they think about him at all? Is he anything more than a holiday on 2 October for them? These were some thoughts the Puffin team wrestled with while *Gandhi Speaks* was taking shape. So in our own little Gandhian way, we decided to give a voice to the intended readers of the book.

Our design team talked to art teachers and came across four students of classes eight and nine of the Mother's International School in New Delhi. Utkarsh Chaturvedi, Tania Saha, Abhishek Negi and Anupriya Roy's art teacher felt they would be able to fulfil our design brief best. Ajanta Guhathakurta, Puffin's head of design says, 'It was a first for us, putting children's artwork on the cover and inside, and I was not sure about whether I would get anything that would live up to our vision of the book.' But the artists were clearly not worried. Armed with a design brief and copies of the manuscript, they executed their ideas about Gandhi and today's child with confidence and style. We got Gandhi with cricket bats, in a playground, with his parents, and Gandhi surrounded by children from various parts of the country. The last has gone on the cover, for its exuberance and because it brought out the idea of the book most evidently. Tania, Abhishek and Anupriya's playful, eyecatching illustrations are inside the book. They serve as reminders that Bapu remains a part of the fabric of our lives.

The Puffin team gratefully acknowledges the enthusiasm and support of the students and teachers of the Mother's International School; Meena Bhat for compiling the quotations; and Keerti Ramachandra for writing the introductions to the chapters. We hope the words and pictures in this book will have the Mahatma speaking to many more children in his own voice.

FOREWORD

I was twelve when Mahatma Gandhi, my grandfather, was killed in Delhi, the city where I lived with my parents, sister Tara, and two brothers, Ramchandra or Ramu and Gopal or Gopu. Though Delhi was not Gandhi's home (in fact for much of his life he had no 'home'), he spent many months in India's capital in the final phase of his life.

Often he stayed with the 'untouchables' (he called them Harijans or Children of God) of the Balmiki community in their colony next to St. Thomas's School on Mandir Marg. At other times he lived as a guest of Ghanshyam Das Birla in Birla House on what is now called Tees January Marg—a new name given to the road after Gandhi's assassination there on 30 January 1948.

My siblings and I were often with him in the Balmiki colony or on the grounds of Birla House, especially for his open-air prayer-meetings, which were held at 5 p.m. On that fateful day, 30 January, however, a sporting event in my school (Modern School) prevented me and my brother Ramu (he was two years younger than me) from joining our grandfather. Returning home from the event, we learnt that he had been shot. Taken to Birla House, we had to fight our way past the large crowds that surrounded it.

We heard before reaching his room that he was dead. Surrounded by flowers, his body lay on a white sheet on the floor. My father Devadas, who was Gandhi's fourth and youngest son, was sitting next to the body, as were my cousins Abha Gandhi and Manu Gandhi, on whose shoulders the Mahatma's arms had rested while he walked to the prayer-site and met the bullets. Also near the body sat Jawaharlal Nehru, India's prime minister, Vallabhbhai Patel, the deputy prime minister, and Lord Mountbatten, independent India's Governor-General.

Everyone was shocked and grieving and yet quite calm. Prayer songs filled the room.

In that room, Bapuji (as I and most Indians of the time called my grandfather) had frequently teased me and my siblings. There he and my youngest brother Gopu, then two, had often made funny faces at each other. Once (this was in Balmiki colony) Bapuji had spotted a new pair of spectacles that I was wearing and asked whether I needed a new frame as well as new lenses. (I was hoping that he would not notice the new glasses but few things escaped him.) Fighting back, I said that he knew my eyes were bad. I think it was a good if incomplete answer.

We were seldom alone with our grandfather. People facing hardships linked to the Partition, and India's new leaders facing daunting responsibilities, had a greater right to his time, and were often with him when we showed up. Though brief, our times with Bapuji were punctuated by hearty laughter from him. He was old and often fasting but his thumps on my back as I bowed to greet him or say goodbye were strong. I recall them to this day, when I am seventy-three.

Narayan Desai, ten years older than me, is the son of Mahadev Desai, who was Gandhi's secretary and companion for twenty-five years. Unlike me (and most of the Mahatma's grandchildren), Narayan spent a lot of time with Bapuji, first in Sabarmati Ashram (near Ahmedabad) and then in the Sevagram Ashram (near Wardha).

XI

One thing that Narayan noticed was the Mahatma's delight in being with children. Putting his hands on the shoulders of the boys, he would lift his feet off the ground and let the youngsters carry him for a while. And if someone had experienced grief, Bapuji would embrace the person 'as if he was absorbing their agony into his own heart'.

His enjoyment of children has been captured for all time in two glorious photographs. One is of him kissing little Nandini, the niece of Pyarelal Nayar, who was also Gandhi's secretary and companion. The other, aptly titled 'The leader led', is of Gandhi running to catch his grandson (and my cousin) Kanu, then about twelve, on the sands of Juhu beach.

Gandhi absorbed others' sorrows and made them his own, and had his own deep disappointments, but he refused to dwell in gloom. A sparkle and a chuckle are inseparable from my images of him.

Why was he able to smile and laugh amidst sadness? Because he was convinced that our universe has been made by the Creator for goodness, happiness, beauty and justice. No doubt we often see badness, sadness, ugliness and injustice, yet these realities are weaker and less durable than their positive opposites. It was from daily experience that Gandhi concluded: 'In the midst of death, life persists; in the midst of untruth, truth persists; in the midst of darkness, light persists.'

It would be an interesting exercise for youngsters (and grown-ups) to ask, what was Gandhi's greatest achievement? He led India to independence, many will say. He certainly did that. British leaders who tried to preserve their country's Empire have acknowledged Gandhi's critical role in its demise.

Jawaharlal Nehru gave a somewhat different answer. Gandhi, he said, removed fear from the hearts of Indians. Others have drawn the same conclusion.

Yet Gandhi was not fearless as a boy. He has told us that he was afraid of the dark, of robbers, of snakes, of ghosts. He has also told us that, by contrast, his wife Kastur (the two were married very young, as was the custom in those days) was naturally brave and quite calm about the things that frightened him.

The discovery that his young bride was braver than him was a big blow to Mohandas Gandhi's male pride. But even in his boyhood and youth Gandhi possessed one remarkable quality: he observed himself. *He recognized that he was afraid.*

To recognize a weakness is to overcome much of it. He acted in spite of his fears, not because he felt no fear. There were steps he felt he had to take (such as presenting a written confession about theft to his ill father). He would take the steps because they were right, not because they felt easy or comfortable.

By monitoring himself, Gandhi was able to do formidable things. While honest about his weaknesses, Gandhi refused to lower his aims. He was confident that God and his compatriots would provide what he lacked but needed to reach his goals.

Because one man who was not naturally fearless obeyed his conscience, the backs of a whole nation were straightened, and their heads were held high.

Though not brave by nature, the boy Mohandas was unusual all right. His autobiography, where Gandhi refers to his timidity as a boy and to episodes of trembling before audiences, is misleading because it does not mention either his strengths or his convictions as a boy.

Those who examine Mohandas's years in Rajkot before he went, as an eighteen-year-old, to study law in England will find that even the teenage Gandhi was troubled by four things: India's subjection to Britain, the Hindu-Muslim divide, the injustice of untouchability, and the hardships of poor Indians. They will find, too, that Mohandas was something of a leader of the students of Rajkot.

Gandhi excludes these aspects of his boyhood from his famous autobiography. If we recognize these features, can we also see them as traces of the future Mahatma?

I do not know. Yet Gandhi seems to have had inklings, even as a boy, of difficult and possibly crucial demands on his life.

One thing is certain: Mohandas was given great love by both his parents. This love, and the trust they had in him, helped produce the confidence that enabled the older Gandhi to confront every threat and challenge.

So the Gandhi story is, among other things, an example of the impact parents can have, apart from also being an example of what an individual who makes up her or his mind can accomplish.

The youngsters who read these pages belong to a world which in many ways is very different from the one of the 1880s that Mohandas faced as a youth in Rajkot and London.

Yet some things are surely similar. Today's youngsters also face troubling realities. Who knows what they will accomplish if they are ready to monitor themselves, if despite weaknesses they are willing to take on large goals, if they are able to make up their minds? May they be inspired by the Gandhi story and by his words in the pages of this book!

New Delhi   Rajmohan Gandhi
January 2009

Parents and Family

A twelve-year-old boy watches, with rapt attention, a group of travelling performers enact the story of Shravan Kumar. On a sling basket fitted across his shoulders, Shravan carries his blind parents on a pilgrimage. During the journey, the boy goes to a river to bring them some water and is accidentally shot dead by King Dasharath. Shravan Kumar's parents are devastated. As they die, they curse the king that he too will die pining for his son.

The twelve-year-old boy had read this story in the only book he possessed other than his textbooks. Although the story had moved him deeply, after he saw the performance he made up his mind to emulate Shravan Kumar and be the ideal son to his parents throughout his life.

This youngster was Mohandas Karamchand Gandhi, whom we now call Mahatma Gandhi or affectionately Bapu, Father of the Nation. We sometimes forget that he too was a young boy once, like any one of us.

The youngest son of Kaba Gandhi and Putlibai, Mohandas grew up in Rajkot, Gujarat. His father moved there when Mohandas was seven years old. Very early in life he learnt to 'carry out the orders of his elders and not question or examine their actions'. As a result, he grew up to be an obedient, dutiful and respectful youth, blind to the faults of his elders. He was naïve and trusting of everybody and tended to believe what they said. Only after several unhappy experiences did he realize that not everyone was as honest and truthful as himself.

From his father, who was not a highly educated man, Mohandas inherited a strong sense of self-respect, loyalty to his community and a passion for truth and justice. Kaba Gandhi was not an ambitious man, with little desire or inclination to accumulate wealth. So though Mohandas's childhood was spent in reasonable comfort, their life was marked by austerity rather than extravagance.

Mohandas's mother was a deeply pious person. She inculcated in him a strong sense of religious discipline not by setting down rules, but by her own example. She was widely respected in the community for her intelligence, knowledge and sound common sense. These three qualities were held in high esteem by Mohandas throughout his life.

When he was still in school, Mohandas was called upon to nurse his ailing father. It was a long and painful illness and Mohandas spent hours before and after school, dressing his father's wound, giving him his medicines, massaging his legs, until Kaba Gandhi fell asleep. Only then would Mohandas retire to his own room and his newly acquired wife. This experience of caring for the sick made him realize that service to humanity not only gave him great satisfaction and joy, it also brought him closer to God.

Mohandas was deeply attached to his older brothers too and fully conscious of the sacrifices they had to make to educate him and then send him to England to study. When he returned, they tried to help him establish a legal practice. Throughout his stay in England Mohandas made sure he maintained a frugal lifestyle so that his brothers were not put to a greater financial burden than necessary. And at the first opportunity he got he offered as much money as he could to repay his brothers' debts.

This sense of obligation, the awareness of what people had done for him gave him a humility and graciousness that later translated into a deep concern and compassion for all humanity. He was able to see divinity in every one of God's creations, so where was the question of hatred or violence against anyone or anything! Instead there was only a firm adherence to the path of peace, love, righteousness, truthfulness, justice and fair play in all his interactions. That is why Rabindranath Tagore gave him the title 'Mahatma'.

My father was a lover of his clan, truthful, brave and generous, but short-tempered. He was incorruptible and had earned a name for strict impartiality in his family as well as outside. His loyalty to the State was well known. An assistant political agent spoke insultingly of the Rajkot Thakore Saheb, Kaba's chief, and he stood up to the insult. The agent was angry and asked Kaba Gandhi to apologize. This he refused to do and was therefore kept under detention for a few hours. But when the agent saw that Kaba Gandhi was adamant, he ordered him to be released.

My father never had any ambition to accumulate riches and left us very little property. He had no education, save that of experience. At best, he might be said to have read up to the fifth Gujarati standard. Of history and geography he was innocent. But his rich experience of practical affairs stood him in good

stead in the solution of the most intricate questions and in managing hundreds of men. Of religious training he had very little, but he had that kind of religious culture which frequent visits to temples and listening to religious discourses make available to many Hindus.
An Autobiography or The Story of My Experiments with Truth
(Abridged), Puffin Classics
(Penguin Books India, 2006, p. 8)

The outstanding impression my mother has left on my memory is that of saintliness. She was deeply religious. She would not think of taking her meals without her daily prayers. Going to Haveli—the Vaishnava temple— was one of her daily duties. She would take the hardest vows and keep them without flinching. Illness was no excuse for relaxing them. To keep two or three consecutive fasts was nothing to her. Living on one meal a day during *Chaturmas* was a habit with her. Not content with that, she fasted every alternate day during one *Chaturmas*. During another *Chaturmas* she vowed not to have food without seeing the sun. We children on those days would stand, staring at the sky, waiting to announce the appearance of the sun to our mother. Everyone knows that at the height of the rainy season the sun often does not condescend to show his face. And I remember days when, at his sudden appearance, we would rush and announce it to her. She would run out to see with her own eyes, but by that time the fugitive sun would be gone, thus depriving her of her meal. 'That does not matter,' she would say cheerfully, 'God did not want me to eat today.' And then she would return to her round of duties.

An Autobiography or The Story of My Experiments with Truth
(Abridged), Puffin Classics
(Penguin Books India, 2006, pp. 8–9)

Somehow my eyes fell on a book purchased by my father. It was *Shravana Pitribhakti Nataka* (a play about Shravana's devotion to his parents). I read it with intense interest. There came to our place about the same time itinerant showmen. One of the pictures I was shown was of Shravana carrying, by means of slings fitted for his shoulders, his blind parents on a pilgrimage. The book and the picture left an indelible impression on my mind. 'Here is an example for you to copy,' I said to myself. The agonized lament of the parents over Shravana's death is still fresh in my memory.

The melting tune moved me deeply, and I played it on a concertina which my father had purchased for me.

An Autobiography or The Story of My Experiments with Truth (*Abridged*), Puffin Classics (Penguin Books India, 2006, pp. 11–12)

There was a similar incident connected with another play. Just about this time, I had secured my father's permission to see a play performed by a certain dramatic company. This play—*Harishchandra*—captured my heart. I could never be tired of seeing it. But how often should I be permitted to go? It haunted me and I must have acted *Harishchandra* to myself times without number. 'Why should not all be truthful like Harishchandra?' was the question I asked myself day and night. To follow truth and to go through all the ordeals Harishchandra went through was the one ideal it inspired in me. I literally believed in the story of Harishchandra. The thought of it all often made me weep. My common sense tells me today that Harishchandra could not have been a historical character. Still both Harishchandra and Shravana are living realities for me, and I am sure

I should be moved as before if I were to read those plays again today.

An Autobiography or The Story of My Experiments with Truth (*Abridged*), Puffin Classics (Penguin Books India, 2006, p. 12)

A relative and I became fond of smoking. Not that we saw any good in smoking, or were enamoured of the smell of a cigarette. We simply imagined a sort of pleasure in emitting clouds of smoke from our mouths. My uncle had the habit, and when we saw him smoking, we thought we should copy his example. But we had no money. So we began pilfering stumps of cigarettes thrown away by my uncle.

The stumps, however, were not always available, and could not emit much smoke either. So we began to steal coppers from the servant's pocket money in order to purchase Indian cigarettes. But the question was where to keep them. We could not of course smoke in the presence of elders. We managed some how for a few weeks on these stolen coppers. In the meantime we heard that the stalks of a certain plant were porous and could be smoked like cigarettes. We got them and began this kind of smoking.

But we were far from being satisfied with such things as these. Our want of independence began to smart. It was unbearable that we should be unable to do anything without the elders' permission. At last, in sheer disgust, we decided to commit suicide!

But how were we to do it? From where were we to get the poison? We heard that Dhatura seeds were an effective poison. Off we went to the jungle in search of these seeds, and got them. Evening was thought to be the auspicious hour. We went to Kedarji Mandir, put ghee in the temple-lamp, had the darshan and then looked for a lonely corner. But our courage failed us. Supposing we were not instantly killed? And what was the good of killing ourselves? Why not rather put up with the lack of independence? But we swallowed two or three seeds nevertheless. We dared not take more. Both of us fought shy of death, and decided to go to Ramji Mandir to compose ourselves, and to dismiss the thought of suicide.

I realized that it was not as easy to commit suicide as to contemplate it. And since then, whenever I have heard of someone threatening to commit suicide, it has had little or no effect on me.

The thought of suicide ultimately resulted in both of us bidding goodbye to the habit of smoking stumps of cigarettes and of stealing the servant's coppers for the purpose of smoking.

Ever since I have grown up, I have never desired to smoke and have always regarded the habit of smoking as barbarous, dirty and harmful. I have never understood why there is such a rage for smoking throughout the world. I cannot bear to travel in a compartment full of people smoking. I become choked.

But much more serious than this theft was the one I was guilty of a little later. I pilfered the coppers when I was twelve or thirteen, possibly less. The other theft was committed when I was fifteen. In this case I stole a bit of gold out of my meat-eating brother's armlet. This brother had run into a debt of about twenty-five rupees. He had on his arm an armlet of solid gold. It was not difficult to clip a bit out of it.

Well, it was done, and the debt cleared. But this became more than I could bear. I resolved never to steal again. I also made up my mind to confess it to my father. But I did not dare to speak. Not that I was afraid of my father beating me. No. I do not recall his ever having beaten any of us. I was afraid of the pain that I should cause him. But I felt that the risk should be taken; that there could not be a cleansing without a clean confession.

I decided at last to write out the confession, to submit it to my father and ask his forgiveness. I wrote it on a slip of paper and handed it to him myself. In this note not only did I confess my guilt, but I asked adequate punishment for it, and closed with a request to him not to punish himself for my offence. I also pledged myself never to steal in future.

I was trembling as I handed the confession to my father. He was then suffering from a fistula and was confined to bed. His bed was a plain wooden plank. I handed him the note and sat opposite the plank.

He read it through, and pearl-drops trickled down his cheeks, wetting the paper. For a moment he closed his eyes in thought and then tore up the note. He had sat up to read it. He again lay down. I also cried. I could see my father's agony. If I were a painter I could draw a picture of the whole scene today. It is still so vivid in my mind.

Those pearl-drops of love cleansed my heart, and washed my sin away. Only he who has experienced such love can know what it is. As the hymn says:

'Only he
Who is smitten with the arrows of love,
Knows its power.'

This was, for me, an object-lesson in *Ahimsa*. Then I could read in it nothing more than a father's love, but today I know that it was pure *Ahimsa*. When such *Ahimsa* becomes all-embracing, it transforms everything it touches. There is no limit to its power.

An Autobiography or The Story of My Experiments with Truth (Abridged), Puffin Classics
(Penguin Books India, 2006, pp. 27–30)

The remedy against cowardice is not physical culture but the braving of dangers. So long as the parents of the middle class Hindus, themselves timid, continue to transmit their timidity by keeping their grown-up children in cotton-wool, so long will there be their desire to shun danger and run no risks. They will have to dare to leave their children alone, let them run risks and even at times get killed in so doing.

Young India, 29 May 1924

There is no school equal to a decent home and no teachers equal to honest, virtuous parents.

Harijan, 8 March 1935

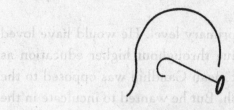

EDUCATION

At Tolstoy Farm, in South Africa, Gandhiji took upon himself the education of all the children living on the farm. His own sons were part of this experiment. Once, when one of his associates questioned the wisdom of Gandhiji's sons spending their days with boys who were rough and 'loafers', Gandhiji was puzzled. He thought over it, and decided that he could not send his sons away from the other children. He was convinced that living in this community they would learn to discriminate between good and bad. Growing up in the midst of children from different backgrounds, they would lose any sense of superiority they might have, and learn to interact with all kinds of children.

One of Gandhiji's primary concerns was education. He believed every child had the right to education. His views on education have influenced many of the policies adopted by the government in independent India. He was convinced that children learn best and quickest if they are taught in the mother-tongue, especially at the primary level. He would have loved to see this continue throughout higher education as well. This did not mean Gandhiji was opposed to the learning of English. But he wanted to inculcate in the youth a sense of pride in their mother-tongues and a respect for all Indian languages. He himself attempted to learn Tamil, Urdu, Hindi, Sanskrit, even Persian and Arabic. The ideal education system, he felt, should train children in body and spirit and not merely teach them the letters. It should also make them self-reliant.

That is why he laid great emphasis on vocational training—the teaching of a traditional craft or skill which would enable young people to earn a living, alongside the formal learning of history, geography and arithmetic. Thus they would beware of exploitation, cheating and deception and have a true sense of their own worth. Had we followed his advice, we would not today bemoan the fact that many of our traditional crafts are dying out, that children are dropping out of schools to help parents in their farms, and that education has come to mean being able to sign one's name. Child rights activists would not have to fight to prevent child labour and to free children forced to sit in front of looms, pump the bellows in a metal foundry or spend their lives making fireworks, instead of being in school.

Gandhiji was rather revolutionary in his attitude towards textbooks. He remembered, during his own schooldays, how he would learn his lessons better if he heard them in the form of stories, rather than when he read them in textbooks. Now, storytelling has become an accepted methodology in education, especially at the primary level. But Gandhiji also thought that learning things by heart was a very good practice to keep the brain sharp and alert. He used to paste verses from the Gita in his house and memorize a verse every day while he was performing his 'daily ablutions'.

Making lessons interesting and stimulating makes great demands on the teacher. But according to Gandhiji, teachers should be prepared to make that extra effort. They should have a very close relationship with their students, and touch the hearts of their pupils. He wanted teachers to teach by example and practise exactly what they preached.

He viewed teachers as trustees of the minds of the pupils, helping them build character, not just imparting dry facts. One of the steps towards building character was the discipline enforced by physical labour. Though Gandhiji himself hated gymnastics and sports when he was in school, he realized later how important it was to be physically fit. That is why he insisted on physical exercise at the farm.

In the early twentieth century it was not common for girls to be given an education, but Gandhiji was determined to include them in all his programmes — be it education or social service, physical training or character building, domestic chores or participating in the freedom struggle. He would have been delighted to see how in today's India, more and more women are benefiting from education and participating in public life.

There is an incident which occurred at the examination during my first year at the high school and which is worth recording. Mr Giles, the educational inspector, had come on a visit of inspection. He had set us five words to write as a spelling exercise. One of the words was 'kettle'. I had misspelt it. The teacher tried to prompt me with the point of his boot, but I would not be prompted. It was beyond me to see that he wanted me to copy the spelling from my neighbour's slate, for I had thought that the teacher was there to supervise us against copying. The result was that all the boys, except myself, were found to have spelt every word correctly. Only I had been stupid. The teacher tried later to bring this stupidity home to me, but without effect. I never could learn the art of 'copying'.

An Autobiography or The Story of My Experiments with Truth (Abridged), Puffin Classics
(Penguin Books India, 2006, p. 11)

There was another such incident during the time when I was in the seventh standard. Dorabji Edulji Gimi was the headmaster then. He was popular among boys, as he was a disciplinarian, a man of method and a good teacher. He had made gymnastics and cricket compulsory for boys of the upper standards. I disliked both. I never took part in any exercise, cricket or football, before they were made compulsory. My shyness was one of the reasons for this aloofness, which I now see was wrong. I then had the false notion that gymnastics had nothing to do with education. Today I know that physical training should have as much place in the curriculum as mental training.

An Autobiography or The Story of My Experiments with Truth (Abridged), Puffin Classics
(Penguin Books India, 2006, p. 18)

My brother had children and my own child was now a boy of nearly four. It was my desire to teach these little ones physical exercise and make them hardy and also to give them the benefit of my personal guidance. In this I had my brother's support and I succeeded in my efforts more or less. I very much liked the company of children and the habit of playing and joking with them has stayed with me till today. I have ever since thought that I should make a good teacher of children.

An Autobiography or The Story of My Experiments with Truth (*Abridged*), Puffin Classics (Penguin Books India, 2006, pp. 62–63)

But though I was none the worse for having neglected exercise, I am still paying the penalty of another neglect. I do not know whence I got the notion that good handwriting was not a necessary part of education, but I retained it until I went to England. When later, especially in South Africa, I saw the beautiful handwriting of lawyers and young men born and educated in South Africa, I was ashamed of myself and repented of my neglect. I saw that bad handwriting should be regarded as a sign of an imperfect education. I tried later to improve mine, but it was too late. I could never repair the neglect of my youth. Let every young man and woman be warned by my example, and understand that good handwriting is a necessary part of education. I am now of the opinion that children should first be taught the art of drawing before learning how to write. Let the child learn his letters by observation as he does different objects, such as flowers, birds, etc., and let him learn handwriting only after he has learnt to draw objects. He will then write a beautifully formed hand.

An Autobiography or The Story of My Experiments with Truth (Abridged), Puffin Classics
(Penguin Books India, 2006, p. 19)

In my scheme of things the hand will handle tools before it draws or traces the writing. The eyes will read the pictures of letters and words as they will know other things in life, the ears will catch the names and meanings of things and sentences. The whole training will be natural, responsive and, therefore, the quickest and the cheapest in the world.

Harijan, 28 August 1937

I hold that true education of the intellect can only come through a proper exercise and training of the bodily organs, for example hands, feet, eyes, ears, nose, etc. In other words an intelligent use of the bodily organs in a child provides the best and easily the quickest way of developing his intellect. But unless the development of the mind and body goes hand in hand with a corresponding awakening of the soul, the former alone would prove to be a poor lopsided affair. By spiritual training I mean education of the heart.

Harijan, 8 May 1937

Literacy in itself is no education. I would therefore begin the child's education by teaching it a useful handicraft, enabling it to produce from the moment it begins its training … I hold that the highest development of the mind and the soul is possible under such a system of education. Only every handicraft has to be taught not merely mechanically as is done today, but scientifically, i.e., the child should know the why and the wherefore of every process.

Harijan, 31 July 1937

It is popularly and correctly described as education through handicrafts. This is part of the truth. The root of this new education goes much deeper. It lies in the application of truth and love in every variety of human activity, whether in individual life or a corporate one. The notion of education through handicrafts rises from the contemplation of truth and love permeating life's activities. Love requires that true education should be easily accessible to all, and should be of use to every villager in his daily life. Such education is not derived from, nor does it depend upon, books. It has no relation to sectional religion. If it can be called religious, it is universal religion from which all sectional religions are derived. Therefore, it is learnt from the Book of Life which costs nothing and which cannot be taken away from one by any force on earth.

Harijan, 21 December 1947

The boys [Gandhi's sons] acquired some knowledge of Gujarati through my conversation and intercourse with them, which was strictly in the mother-tongue. I was loath to send them back to India for I believed even then that young children should not be separated from their parents. The education that children naturally imbibe in a well-ordered household is impossible to obtain in hostels. I therefore kept my children with me.

An Autobiography
(Navajivan Publishing House, 1927, p. 184)

I did not believe in the existing system of education, and I had a mind to find out by experience and experiment the true system. Only this much I knew—that under ideal conditions, true education could be imparted only by the parents, and that then there should be a minimum of outside help, that Tolstoy Farm was a family, in which I occupied the place of the father, and that I should so far as possible shoulder the responsibility for the training of the young.

An Autobiography or The Story of My Experiments with Truth (*Abridged*), Puffin Classics
(Penguin Books India, 2006, pp. 176–77)

English is today admittedly the world language. I would therefore accord it a place as a second, optional language, not in school, but in the university course.

That can only be for the select few — not for the millions . . . It is our mental slavery that makes us feel that we cannot do without English. I can never subscribe to that defeatist creed.

Harijan, 25 August 1946

I must not be understood to decry English or its noble literature. The columns of the *Harijan* are sufficient evidence of my love of English. But the nobility of its literature cannot avail the Indian nation any more than the temperate climate or the scenery of England can avail her. India has to flourish in her own climate and scenery, and her own literature, even though all the three may be inferior to the English climate, scenery and literature. We and our children must build on our own heritage. If we borrow another, we impoverish our own. We can never grow on foreign victuals. I want the nation to have the treasures contained in that language and, for that matter, in other languages of the world, through its own vernaculars. I do not need to learn Bengali in order to know the beauties of Rabindranath's matchless productions. I get them through good translations. Gujarati boys and girls do not need to learn Russian to appreciate Tolstoy's short stories. They learn them through good translations. It is the boast of Englishmen that the best of the world's literary output is in the hands of that nation in simple English inside of a week of its publication. Why need I learn English to get at the best of what Shakespeare and Milton thought and wrote?

Harijan, 9 July 1938

I do not want my house to be walled in on all sides and my windows to be stuffed. I want the cultures of all lands to be blown about my house as freely as possible. But I refuse to be blown off my feet by any.

Young India, 1 June 1921

I believe implicitly that the child is not born mischievous in the bad sense of the term. If parents behave themselves whilst the child is growing, before it is born and after, it is a well-known fact that the child would instinctively obey the law of Truth and the law of Love . . .

[These words are part of his speech at the Montessori Training College and printed in *Young India*, 19 November 1931]

Knowledge without character is a power for evil only, as seen in the instances of so many 'talented thieves' and 'gentlemen rascals' in the world.

Young India, 21 February 1929

If we are to reach real peace in this world and we are to carry on a real war against war, we shall have to begin with children; and if they will grow up in their natural innocence, we won't have to struggle, we won't have to pass fruitless idle resolutions. But we shall go from love to love and peace to peace, until at last all the corners of the world are covered with that peace and love for which, consciously or unconsciously, the whole world is hungering.

Young India, 19 November 1931

Persistent questioning and healthy inquisitiveness are the first requisites for acquiring learning of any kind. Inquisitiveness should be tempered by humility and respectful regard for the teacher. It must not degenerate into impudence. The latter is the enemy of the receptivity of the mind. There can be no knowledge without humility and the will to learn.

Harijan, 8 September 1946

We are living in times when values are undergoing quick changes. We are not satisfied with slow results. We are not satisfied with the welfare merely of our own caste-fellows, not even of our own country. We feel or want to feel for the whole of humanity. All this is a tremendous gain in humanity's search towards its goal.

Harijan, 30 May 1937

Students should have the greatest freedom of expression and of opinion . . . be an active politician and pursue his studies at the same time

Harijan, 2 October 1937

I know that they (students) waste a great deal of time in idleness. By strict economy they can save hours . . . I would therefore advise patriotic students to lose one year, not at a stretch, but spread it over their whole study. They will find that one year so given will not be a waste of time. The effort will add to their equipment, mental, moral and physical, and they will have made even during their studies, a substantial contribution to the freedom movement.

The Bombay Chronicle, 9 January 1946

Students must become pioneers in conservative reform, conserving all that is good in the nation and fearlessly ridding society of the innumerable abuses that have crept into it . . . students in olden times were called Brahmacharis, that is those who walked with and in the fear of God. They were honoured by Kings and elders. They were a voluntary charge on the nation and in return they gave to the nation a hundred-fold strong souls, strong brains, strong arms. Students in the modern world, wherever they are to be found among fallen nations, are considered to be their hope, and have become the self-sacrificing leaders of reforms in every department. Not that we have no such examples in India; but they are far too few.

Young India, 9 June 1927

The students should devote the whole of their vacation to village service ... The village work I have mentioned is easily the best form of recreation and light instruction.

Young India, 26 December 1929

People think one ceases to be a student when his school days are over. With me it is the other way about. I hold that so long as I live, I must have a student's inquiring mind and thirst for learning.

Manu Gandhi's Diary, 2 February 1947

28

GRAHAM SPEAKS

But it is that simple? Does one have to be truthful only
if one is in danger of being found out?

In the second instance, when you are in charge and
you know some wrong has been done, should't you
speak up? By keeping quiet, aren't you covering for his
mistake? Even if you know that you will probably get

TRUTHFULNESS AND TRUTH

Imagine: A cricket field. You are the last man in. Your
team is depending on you to get the runs and win the
match. Your heart is hammering in your chest, sweat
pours down your helmet as you concentrate on the ball.
The bowler charges down, the ball rises sharply and
within moments, the wicketkeeper, the close-in fielders
and the bowler leap up screaming, 'How's that!' You
instinctively turn around, and then look back at the
umpire. He seems uncertain. But you know you nicked
the ball. What do you do?

Imagine: The class bully has broken a windowpane.
The teacher, convinced it's him, questions you as the
monitor, asks you to tell her who did it. The bully is
glaring at you. What do you do? Tell on him? Or keep
quiet?

These situations are examples of the same dilemma —
being truthful versus being dishonest. In the first
instance, you can say there was an umpire to decide
whether you were out or not, so why should you walk?

But is it that simple? Does one have to be truthful only if one is in danger of being found out?

In the second instance, when you are in charge and you know some wrong has been done, shouldn't you speak up and let the wrong-doer be punished for his mistake? Even if you know that you will probably get beaten up later? Or lose your popularity and be called a tale carrier, a sneak, by your classmates?

These are simple everyday situations that we find ourselves in. And learning how to deal with them is an act of character-building. Being truthful not only means admitting to one's mistake, but also means not keeping silent when one knows the truth. It also means not letting other people, even if they are older or in authority, force you into doing something wrong.

Gandhiji talks about this at length in his autobiography. He exhorts everyone to make truthfulness a habit from the earliest years of one's life.

It is not all that easy to be truthful. We have read how Gandhi confessed to his father about stealing money from home, and how his father's silent reproach affected him so deeply and made him feel so ashamed of himself, he vowed never to steal or tell a lie again. This pledge, to be scrupulously honest and truthful, Gandhiji kept even when he was a practising lawyer in South Africa. He was severely tested on many occasions, but never compromised on the truth. In one instance, though Gandhiji won the case for his client, he suspected that the client had lied to him. The victory gave him no satisfaction.

Gandhiji advocated truthfulness at all times, in all aspects of one's own life and in all one's dealings with others. He believed that if one is truthful:

- One will not do any wrong.
- One will be willing to face the consequences of one's actions. It means one is not a coward.
- One can fight for any cause because that cause can only be legitimate.
- One can overcome any adversary.
- One is honest, has integrity, courage . . . all attributes of a strong moral character.

Gandhiji wanted to evolve a set of guiding principles upon which he could base his life and all his activities. He realized that it was the principle of truthfulness that was the most fundamental. That would, in turn, help him understand the meaning of life, religion, philosophy and God.

As father of, you might say, many boys and girls, you might also say of thousands of boys and girls, I want to tell you, boys, that after all you hold your destiny in your own hands. I do not care what you learn or what you do not learn in your school, if you will observe two conditions. One condition is that you must be fearlessly truthful against the heaviest odds under every circumstance imaginable. A truthful boy, a brave boy will never think of hurting even a fly. He will defend all the weak boys in his school and help, whether inside school or outside, all those who need his help.

A chivalrous boy would always keep his mind pure, his eyes straight and his hands unpolluted. You do not need to go to any school to learn these fundamental maxims of life, and if you will have this triple character with you, you will build on a strong foundation.

With Gandhiji in Ceylon, p. 109, this extract from *India of My Dreams*, Rajpal & Sons, 2008

I worship God as Truth, only I have not yet found Him, but I am seeking after Him. I am prepared to sacrifice the things dearest to me in pursuit of this quest. Even if the sacrifice demanded be my very life, I hope I may be prepared to give it. But as long as I have not realized this Absolute Truth, so long must I hold by the relative truth as I have conceived it. That relative truth must, meanwhile, be my beacon, my shield and buckler. Though this path is strait [sic] and narrow and sharp as the razor's edge, for me it has been the quickest and easiest. Even my Himalayan blunders have seemed trifling to me because I have kept strictly to this path. For the path has saved me from coming to grief, and I have gone forward according to my light. Often in my progress I have had faint glimpses of the Absolute Truth, God, and daily the conviction is growing upon me that He alone is real and all else is unreal.

An Autobiography
(Navajivan Publishing House, 1927, p. xiii–xiv)

I have no God to serve but Truth.

Harijan, 15 April 1939

I have no strength except what comes from insistence on truth. Non-violence, too, springs from the same insistence.

Harijan, 7 April 1946

Truth resides in every human heart . . .

Harijan, 10 November 1946

Truth never damages a cause that is just.

Harijan, 10 November 1946

Truth alone will endure, all the rest will be swept away before the tide of time. I must, therefore, continue to bear testimony to Truth even if I am forsaken by all. Mine today may be a voice in the wilderness, but it will be heard when all other voices are silenced, if it is the voice of Truth.

Harijan, 25 August 1946

By Tania Saha, Class IX
The Mother's International School, New Delhi

To me God is Truth and Love; God is ethics and morality; God is fearlessness. God is the source of Light and Life and yet He is above and beyond all these. God is conscience. He is even the atheism of the atheist. For in His boundless love God permits the atheist to live. He is the searcher of hearts. He transcends speech and reason. He knows us and our hearts better than we do ourselves.

Young India, 5 March 1925

God is Truth, but God is many other things also. That is why I say Truth is God . . . Only remember that Truth is not one of the many qualities we name. It is the living embodiment of God, it is the only Life, and I identify Truth with the fullest life, and that is how it becomes a concrete thing, for God is His whole creation, the whole Existence, and service of all that exists — Truth — is service of God.

Harijan, 25 May 1935

I see and find Beauty in Truth or through Truth. All Truths, not merely true ideas, but truthful faces, truthful pictures, or songs, are highly beautiful. People generally fail to see Beauty in Truth, the ordinary man runs away from it and becomes blind to the beauty in it. Whenever men begin to see Beauty in Truth, then true Art will arise.

Young India, 13 November 1924

THE CHARKHA AND KHADI

Have you ever seen a charkha? It is an ancient Indian spinning wheel, used to weave cloth. Many pictures of Gandhiji show him spinning at the charkha. The charkha also featured on the Indian National Congress Party's flag.

While the charkha has been a part of Indian households since Vedic times, it was Gandhiji who made it a mark of his philosophy of non-violence, self-reliance and India's desire for independence.

It was the year 1921. Gandhiji wanted to give the people of India a symbol to revive their faith in the struggle for freedom. At that time, Indian markets were flooded with vast quantities of mill-made foreign cloth, which everyone was buying. Poor weavers were being deprived of their livelihood. By chance Gandhiji came upon the charkha. He thought it was the perfect symbol. It was a machine based on simple technology, and could be used by everyone. It had the potential to give millions employment. It did not exploit natural resources nor human labour. And it gave the spinner a sense of dignity and self-respect.

Gandhiji also encouraged the use of khadi—which was different from handloom fabric in that the yarn from which khadi was woven was also hand-spun. Handloom fabric was woven on looms but using mill-made yarn. The making of khadi involved several other professionals as well. The carder cleaned and combed the cotton before it could be spun into thread on the charkha, then the yarn was dyed and sent to the bobbin winder, warper, sizer and finally to the weaver. The weaver wove the coarse rough cloth called khaddar or khadi into dhotis, shirts and saris. Operating the charkha to spin thread was primarily done by women in villages, while the weaving was invariably the job of the men.

Wearing khadi not only showed the wearer's support of the village economy and of indigenously manufactured goods, but also became a unifying factor across the country.

Ironically, today, khadi has changed its character. It is no longer the poor man's dhoti and kurta. Khadi has become much more versatile—it is dyed and printed, embroidered and embellished into dress materials, furnishing fabrics, bed and bath linen, and even exclusive saris, not to mention the ever popular and trendy khadi kurta pyjamas. You might even spot fashion models wear it as they walk the ramp in fashion shows!

Would Gandhiji be unhappy to see how khadi has changed? Probably not. Because even today the manufacture of khadi is providing sustenance to millions of India's rural population. It was Gandhiji's dream to see the gap between India's rich and poor reduce. If we were to draw a figure to show how India's wealth is divided, we would come up with an isosceles triangle — the broad base representing India's poor, tapering off to a point that represents the extremely wealthy. The distance between the apex and the base was what caused intense grief to Gandhiji. He wanted to see a more plateau-like structure with not much difference between the base and the top. The only way to achieve this, he felt, was to make villages self-reliant, independent and free from exploitation by their urban brethren whom they supported and were partially dependent on. One of the means of achieving this self-reliance was to produce all that one needed locally, using available resources.

Gandhiji's vision has led numerous agencies to work in rural areas, and encourage sustainable development through the formation of cooperative societies.

By Abhishek Negi, Class VIII
The Mother's International School, New Delhi

But there is a responsibility of the city dwellers too. In exchange for what they receive from the villages, they should, with their education, knowledge and exposure to developments in the world, offer their services in the areas of education, health care, agricultural practices. They should also provide information about trends and demands in the outside world and marketing strategies for the villagers' produce. Mutual dependence, cooperation, giving and sharing are the only way by which all of us can live in peace and harmony.

The conviction dawned upon me even before I came to India that the revival of hand-spinning alone could restore India to its pristine glory. I have since compared the spinning-wheel to the central sun round which the solar system of our village economy revolves. It provides the golden bridge between the rich and the poor.

Harijan, 21 July 1946

The message of the spinning-wheel is really to replace the spirit of exploitation by the spirit of service. The dominant note in the West is the note of exploitation. I have no desire that our country should copy that spirit or that note.

Young India, 2 February 1928

The spinning-wheel represents to me the hope of the masses. The masses lost their freedom, such as it was, with the loss of the Charkha. The Charkha supplemented the agriculture of the villagers and gave it dignity. It was the friend and solace of the widow. It kept the villagers from idleness. For the Charkha included all the anterior and posterior industries — ginning, carding, warping, sizing, dyeing and weaving. These in turn kept the village carpenter and the blacksmith busy.

The Charkha enabled seven hundred thousand villages to become self-contained. With the exit of the Charkha went the other village industries, such as the oil press. Nothing took the place of these industries. Therefore, the villages were drained of their varied occupations and their creative talent and what little wealth these brought them. Hence if the villages are to come into their own, the most natural thing that suggests itself is the revival of the Charkha and all it means.

Harijan, 13 April 1940

∽◦⌒

I have no doubt in my mind that the wheel can serve as the instrument of earning one's livelihood and, at the same time, enable the worker to render useful service to his neighbours. In order to ply the wheel intelligently, he should know all the processes that precede and succeed spinning.

Harijan, 17 March 1946

∽◦⌒

In seeking to revive such village industries as are capable of being revived . . . I am trying to do what every lover of village life, everyone who realizes the tragic meaning of the disintegration of villages is doing or trying to do. Why am I turning back the course of modern civilization when I ask the villager to grind his own meal, eat it whole, including the nourishing bran, or when I ask him to turn his sugarcane into gur for his own requirements, if not for sale? Am I turning back the course of modern civilization when I ask the villagers not merely to grow raw produce, but to turn it into marketable products and thereby add a few more pies to their daily income?

Harijan, 4 January 1935

The revival of the village is possible only when it is no more exploited. Industrialization on a mass scale will necessarily lead to passive or active exploitation of the villagers as the problems of competition and marketing come in. Therefore we have to concentrate on the village being self-contained, manufacturing mainly for use. Provided this character of the village industry is maintained, there would be no objection to villagers using even the modern machines and tools that they can make and can afford to use. Only they should not be used as a means of exploitation of others.

Harijan, 28 September 1946

The world is weary of the after-effects of the War. Even as the Charkha is India's comforter today, it may be the world's tomorrow, because it stands not for the greatest good of the greatest number, but for the greatest good of all.

Young India, 10 February 1927

We do not want to universalize the Charkha through mass production in one place. Our ideal is to make the Charkha and all its accessories in the locality where the spinner lives. Therein lies the value of the spinning-wheel. Anything that goes wrong with it should be put right on the spot and the spinners should be taught how to do so.

Harijan, 20 October 1946

I . . . claim for the Charkha the honour of being able to solve the problem of economic distress in a most natural, simple, inexpensive and business-like manner . . . It is the symbol of the nation's prosperity and, therefore, freedom. It is a symbol not of commercial war but of commercial peace.

Young India, 8 December 1921

I can only think of spinning as the fittest and most acceptable sacrificial body labour. I cannot imagine anything nobler or more national than that for, say one hour in the day, we should all labour that the poor must do, and thus identify ourselves with them and through them with all mankind. I cannot imagine better worship of God than that in His name I should labour for the poor even as they do. The spinning-wheel spells a more equitable distribution of riches of the earth.

Young India, 20 October 1921

He who spins before the poor, inviting them to do likewise, serves God as no one else does . . . Spinning is the greatest prayer, the greatest worship, the greatest sacrifice.

Young India, 24 September 1925

[Spinning]
- Requires practically no outlay of capital.
- The wheel can be easily and cheaply made. Most of us do not yet know that spinning can be done even with a piece of tile and splinter.

- It alone can stop the drain of wealth which goes outside India in the purchase of foreign cloth.
- It affords immediate relief in times of famine and scarcity.
- It is the most potent instrument of securing immediate gain among the people

Young India, 21 August 1924

Khaddar is a living thing. But India has lost her eye for the real art and is, therefore, satisfied with the glossy exterior. Revive the healthy national taste for khaddar and you will find every village a busy hive. As it is, the resources of khaddar organizations are taxed to the utmost, in order to create a market for the article . . . The marvel is that, in spite of heavy odds against it, the movement is making headway.

I have thus summarized the case for the spinning-wheel as a supplementary industry as against the handloom. Let there be no confusion of thought. I am not against the handloom. It is a great and thriving industry. It will progress automatically if the spinning-wheel succeeds. It is bound to die if the wheel fails.

Young India, 11 November 1926

By Anupriya Roy, Class IX
The Mother's International School, New Delhi

Economic equality is the master key to non-violent independence. Working for economic equality means abolishing the eternal conflict between capital and labour. It means the levelling down of the few rich in whose hands is concentrated the bulk of the nation's wealth on the one hand, and the levelling up of the semi-starved naked millions on the other.

A non-violent system of government is clearly an impossibility, so long as the wide gulf between the rich and the hungry millions persists . . .

A violent and bloody revolution is a certainty one day unless there is a voluntary abdication of riches and the power that riches give and sharing them for the common good.

Constructive Programme: Its Meaning and Place
(Navajivan Publishing House, Ahmedabad, 1948, pp. 20–21)

Supposing I have come by a fair amount of wealth — either by way of legacy, or by means of trade and industry — I must know that all that wealth does not belong to me; what belongs to me is the right to an honourable livelihood, no better than that enjoyed by millions of others. The rest of my wealth belongs to the community and must be used for the welfare of the community.

Harijan, 3 June 1939

It is true that generally the rich spend more on themselves than they need . . . the well-to-do should educate and bring up their children so that they may learn how to be independent. The tragedy is that they do not do so. Their children do get some education, they even recite verses in praise of poverty, but they have no compunction about helping themselves to parental wealth.

Harijan, 12 April 1942

I do not believe that industrialization is necessary in any case for any country. It is much less so for India. Indeed, I believe that independent India can only discharge her duty towards a groaning world by adopting a simple but ennobled life by developing her thousands of cottage industries and living at peace with the world.

Whether such plain living is possible for an isolated nation, however large geographically and numerically, in the face of a world armed to the teeth and in the midst of pomp and circumstance is a question open to the doubt of a sceptic. The answer is straight and simple. If plain living is worth living, then the attempt is worth making, even though only an individual or group makes the effort.

Harijan, 1 September 1946

My opposition to machinery is much misunderstood. I am not opposed to machinery as such. I am opposed to machinery which displaces labour and leaves it idle.

Harijan, 19 September 1946

SATYAGRAHA AND AHIMSA

Gandhiji developed his philosophy of Satyagraha between 1906 and 1914 when he lived in South Africa. Gandhiji was deeply troubled by the mistreatment of non-whites in South Africa and was appalled by the racial injustices prevailing there. He decided to fight for a more humane treatment of the Indian population and other coloured people. His reading of great literature, study of the religions of the world, and meetings with people from different walks of life convinced him of the truth of the Biblical saying, 'An eye for an eye makes the whole world blind.' Only universal love and goodwill towards all can bring about a change of heart in the most stubborn adversary, he realized. And this led him to practise passive or non-violent resistance. But Gandhiji was not happy with the limited meaning of passive resistance because it was taken to mean 'a weapon of the weak'. It could be characterized by hatred and, most importantly, it would finally manifest itself in violence. A new word was needed to describe the movement or struggle. So Gandhiji asked people for their suggestions through the newspaper *Indian Opinion*, inviting readers to come up with a word or expression. It was Maganlal Gandhi (no relation of the Mahatma's) who suggested the word 'sadagraha'. Gandhiji modified it to satya (truth) + agraha (force).

Not only was Gandhiji very clear about how, where and when Satyagraha was to be practised, he was very particular about who could become a Satyagrahi.

So what did a Satyagrahi have to commit to?

- A Satyagrahi had to honestly try to understand his opponent's point of view.
- A Satyagrahi had to promise never to resort to violence, no matter what the provocation.
- The Satyagrahi had to have boundless patience and try to bring about a change of heart in or the mindset of his oppressor through love and compassion.
- The Satyagrahi had to be prepared to undergo any amount of suffering and hardship until his goal was reached.

In order to be able to fulfil these conditions a Satyagrahi had to have a strong sense of self-discipline, especially when he adopted Gandhiji's most potent weapon, the fast.

By using Satyagraha Gandhiji first fought injustice in South Africa, and after his return to India, used it in India's struggle for independence. But Gandhiji also used satyagraha in less complex and more humble situations to resolve conflict and bring about a change of heart among his family members and colleagues.

Satyagraha, when used judiciously and sincerely, is a potent weapon to obtain justice, be it in the personal or the public domain. Can you think of ways to use it in your life to make changes around you?

A Satyagrahi obeys the laws of society intelligently and of his own free will, because he considers it to be his sacred duty to do so. It is only when a person has thus obeyed the laws of society scrupulously that he is in a position to judge as to which particular laws are good and just and which unjust and iniquitous. Only then does the right accrue to him of civil disobedience of certain laws in well-defined circumstances.

An Autobiography
(Navajivan Publishing House, 1927, p. 347)

In the application of Satyagraha, I discovered, in the earliest stages, that pursuit of Truth did not admit of violence being inflicted on one's opponent, but that he must be weaned from error by patience and sympathy. For, what appears to be truth to the one may appear to be error to the other. And patience means self-suffering. So the doctrine came to mean vindication of Truth, not by infliction of suffering on the opponent but one's own self.

> Report of the Commission Appointed by the Punjab
> Subcommittee of the Indian National Congress
> (published by K. Santhanam, Lahore, 1920)

Fasting is a potent weapon in the Satyagraha armoury. It cannot be taken by every one. Mere physical capacity to take it is no qualification for it. It is of no use without a living faith in God. It should never be a mechanical effort or a mere imitation. It must come from the depth of one's soul. It is, therefore, always rare.

Harijan, 18 March 1939

Ridiculous fasts spread like [the] plague and are harmful. But, when fasting becomes a duty, it cannot be given up. Therefore I do fast when I consider it to be necessary and cannot abstain from it on any score. What I do myself I cannot prevent others from doing under similar circumstances. It is common knowledge that the best of good things are often abused. We see this happening every day.

Harijan, 21 April 1946

Each individual must be taught the art of self-defence. It is more a mental state that has to be inculcated than that our bodies should be trained for retaliation. Our mental training has been one of feeling helpless. Bravery is not a quality of the body, it is of the soul. I have seen cowards encased in tough muscle, and rare courage in the frailest body . . . The weakest of us physically must be taught the art of facing dangers and giving a good account of ourselves.

Young India, 20 November 1921

There is no bravery greater than a resolute refusal to bend the knee to an earthly power, no matter how great, and that, without bitterness of spirit and in the fullness of faith that the spirit alone lives, nothing else does.

Harijan, 15 October 1938

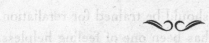

A Satyagrahi is nothing if not instinctively law-abiding, and it is his law-abiding nature which exacts from him implicit obedience to the highest law, that is the voice of conscience which overrides all other laws.

Speeches & Writings of Mahatma Gandh
(G.A. Natesan & Co., 1933, 4th edition)

It is often forgotten that it is never the intention of a Satyagrahi to embarrass the wrong-doer. The appeal is never to his fear; it is, must be, always to his heart. The Satyagrahi's object is to convert, not to coerce, the wrong-doer. He should avoid artificiality in all his doings. He acts naturally and from inward conviction.

Harijan, 24 March 1939

It is not because I value life low that I countenance with joy thousands voluntarily losing their lives for Satyagraha, but because I know that it results, in the long run, in the least loss of life and, what is more, it ennobles those who lose their lives and morally enriches the world for their sacrifice.

Young India, 8 October 1925

Life itself involves some kind of violence and we have to choose the path of least violence.

Harijan, 28 September 1934

Non-violence is a power which can be wielded equally by all—children, young men and women or grown-up people, provided they have a living faith in the God of Love and have therefore equal love for all mankind. When non-violence is accepted as the law of life, it must pervade the whole being and not be applied to isolated acts . . .

Non-violence is the law of the human race . . . it does not avail those who do not possess a living faith in the

God of Love . . . [it] is of no assistance in the defence of ill-gotten gains and immoral acts . . . it is inconsistent with the possession of other people's countries.

Harijan, 5 September 1936

[A living faith in non-violence] is impossible without a living faith in God. A non-violent man can do nothing save by the power and grace of God. Without it he won't have the courage to die without anger, without fear and without retaliation. Such courage comes from the belief that God sits in the hearts of all and that there should be no fear in the presence of God. The knowledge of the omnipresence of God also means respect for the lives even of those who may be called opponents.

Harijan, 18 June 1938

[Barisaheb]° assured me that there was warrant enough for Satyagraha in the Holy Koran. He

_____

°Maulana Abdul Bori Saheb

agreed with the interpretation of the Koran to the effect that, whilst violence under certain well-defined circumstances is permissible, self-restraint is dearer to God than violence, and that is the law of love. That is Satyagraha. Violence is concession to human weakness, Satyagraha is an obligation. Even from a practical standpoint it is easy enough to see that violence can do no good and only do infinite harm.

Young India, 14 May 1919

The path of true non-violence requires much more courage than violence.

Harijan, 4 August 1946

Without ahimsa it is not possible to see and find Truth. Ahimsa and Truth are so intertwined that it is practically impossible to disentangle and separate them. They are like the two sides of a coin, or rather of a smooth, unstamped, metallic disc. Who can say which is the obverse, and which the reverse? Nevertheless ahimsa is the means; Truth is the end. Means to be means must always be within our reach, and so ahimsa is our supreme duty. If we take care of the means, we are bound to reach the end sooner or later. When once we have grasped this point, final victory is beyond question.

Yeravada Mandir: Ashram Observances of Mahatma Gandhi, translated by V.G. Desai (Navajivan Publishing House, 1951, p. 1213)

Thus Satyagraha is a process of educating public opinion, such that it covers all the elements of society and in the end makes itself irresistible. Violence interrupts the process and prolongs the real revolution of the whole social structure.

The conditions necessary for the success of Satyagraha are:

1) The Satyagrahi should not have any hatred in his heart against the opponent.

2) The issue must be true and substantial.

3) The Satyagrahi must be prepared to suffer till the end for his cause.

Harijan, 31 March 1946

Strength does not come from physical capacity. It comes from an indomitable will.

Young India, 11 August 1920

I learnt the lesson of non-violence from my wife, when I tried to bend her to my will. Her determined resistance to my will, on the one hand, and her quiet submission to the suffering my stupidity involved on the other, ultimately made me ashamed of myself and cured me of my stupidity in thinking that I was born to rule over her, and in the end she became my teacher in non-violence.

Harijan, 24 December 1938

It is the acid test of non-violence that, in a non-violent conflict, there is no rancour left behind, and in the end the enemies are converted into friends. That was my experience in South Africa, with General Smuts.* He

---

*General Smuts, South African politician and statesman, Minister of Interior when Gandhi proposed Satyagraha in South Africa, later Prime Minister of Union of South Africa.

started with being my bitterest opponent and critic. Today he is my warmest friend.

Harijan, 12 November 1938

Satyagraha is soul force pure and simple, and whenever and to whatever extent there is room for the use of arms or physical force or brute force, there and to that extent is there so much less possibility for soul force.

Satyagraha in South Africa
(Navajivan Publishing House, 1928, p. 113)

Violence is like water when it has an outlet, rushes forward furiously with an overwhelming force. Non-violence cannot act madly. It is the essence of discipline. But when it is set going, no amount of violence can crush it. For full play, it requires unsullied purity and an unquenchable faith.

Harijan, 21 March 1939

64

I object to violence because when it appears to do good, the good is only temporary; the evil it does is permanent ... The true meaning of non-resistance has often been misunderstood or even distorted. It never implies that a non-violent man should bend before the violence of an aggressor. While not returning the latter's violence by violence, he should refuse to submit to the latter's illegitimate demand even to the point of death. That is the true meaning of non-resistance.

Harijan, 15 April 1939

If one has not the courage, I want him to cultivate the art of killing and being killed, rather than in a cowardly manner flee from danger.

Harijan, 15 January 1938.

My non-violence is not merely kindness to all living creatures. The emphasis laid on the sacredness of sub-human life in Jainism is understandable. But that can never mean that one is to be kind in this life in preference to human life. While writing about the sacredness of such life, I take it that the sacredness of human life has been taken for granted. The former has been over-emphasized. And while putting it into practice, the idea has undergone distortion. For instance, there are many who derive complete satisfaction in feeding ants. It would appear that the theory has become a wooden, lifeless dogma. Hypocrisy and distortion are passing current under the name of religion.

Ahimsa is the highest ideal. It is meant for the brave, never the cowardly. To benefit by others' killing and delude oneself into the belief that one is being very religious and non-violent is sheer self-deception.

Harijan, 9 June 1946

My non-violence does not admit of running away from danger and leaving dear ones unprotected. Between violence and cowardly flight, I can only prefer violence to cowardice. I can no more preach non-violence to a coward than I can tempt a blind man to enjoy healthy scenes. Non-violence is the summit of bravery. And in my own experience I have had no difficulty in demonstrating to men trained in the school of violence the superiority of non-violence. As a coward, which I was for years, I harboured violence. I began to prize non-violence only when I began to shed cowardice.

Young India, 28 May 1924

The science of non-violence can alone lead one to pure democracy.

Harijan, 15 October 1938

I admit that the strong will rob the weak and that it is sin to be weak. But this is said of the soul in man, not of the body. If it be said of the body, we could never be free from the sin of weakness. But the strength of the soul can defy a whole world in arms against it. This strength is open to the weakest in body.

Young India, 6 May 1926

A small body of determined spirits fired by an unquenchable faith in their mission can alter the course of history.

Young India, 6 May 1926

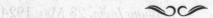

Violence is needed for the protection of things external, non-violence is needed for the protection of the Atman, for the protection of one's honour.

Harijan, 1 September 1940

Nothing but organized non-violence can check the organized violence of the British Empire.

In a letter written to Lord Irwin, the then Viceroy, announcing his decision to break the Salt Law

Truth can never be propagated by doing violence. Those who believe in the justice of their cause have need to possess boundless patience and those alone are

fit to offer civil disobedience, who are above committing criminal disobedience or doing violence.

Young India, 28 April 1920

Satyagraha is a relentless search for truth and a determination to reach truth.

Young India, 19 March 1925

Non-violence in its dynamic condition means conscious suffering. It does not mean meek submission to the will of the evil-doer, but it means the pitting of one's whole soul against the will of the tyrant. Working under this law of our being, it is possible for a single individual to defy the whole might of an unjust empire to save his honour, his religion, his soul and lay the foundation for that empire's fall or regeneration.

Young India, 1 August 1920

The very frightfulness of the atom bomb will not force non-violence on the world. If all the nations are armed with the atom bomb, they will refrain from using it as it will mean absolute destruction for all concerned? I am of the opinion that it will not. The violent man's eye would be lit up with the prospect of the much greater amount of destruction and death which he could now wreak.

Harijan, 23 July 1946

When India becomes self-supporting, self-reliant, and proof against temptations and exploitation, she will cease to be the object of greedy attraction for any power in the West or the East and will then feel secure without having to carry the burden of expensive armaments. Her internal economy will be the strongest bulwark against aggression.

Young India, 2 July 1931

THE COOPERATIVE MOVEMENT AND SELF-RELIANCE

All of us are familiar with the utterly butterly delicious Amul butter, cheese, ice cream, chocolates and other milk products available in the market. But how many of us have looked at the wrapper to see who makes these excellent products? They are not made by a multinational company, or a big food processing giant, but by a milk producers' cooperative society in Gujarat. It has changed the lives of small and medium dairy farmers who used to depend on their own marketing skills to sell their produce. Earlier, besides vagaries of the weather, variations in demand and problems related to delivery often left the milkman with quantities of unsold milk. As a result he was not assured of a steady income and often found himself in debt. Or he had to rely on the middleman to buy all his produce, and was often cheated and exploited in the process.

However, all this changed when the idea of starting a 'cooperative society' was suggested to clusters of villages. They were persuaded to pool in their produce, follow a strategy for marketing their product so that they were assured of a fair price, and did not have to individually find customers or deliver at doorsteps. The idea caught on and gradually cooperative societies became more professionally managed. Today, Amul represents the exemplary success of the cooperative movement.

The cooperative movement is very strong in the areas of microfinance, banking, agriculture, food production, distribution and processing industries, and has benefited large rural communities. Even in urban areas, cooperative housing societies are very common and popular.

It was Gandhiji who introduced the idea of the cooperative movement in India. He firmly believed that cooperation was the gateway to economic freedom. He had experimented with it in South Africa as early as 1904 when he established the Phoenix Settlement after reading John Ruskin's *Unto This Last*. In this book Ruskin talks about the virtues of the simple life of love and labour and the dignity of human beings. All three ideas were very close to Gandhiji's heart.

Later on, he read more extensively the works of Leo Tolstoy, David Henry Thoreau and the Bhagvad Gita. Tolstoy spoke about renouncing violence as a means of opposition, Thoreau gave him the idea of civil disobedience and from the Gita he learnt that selfless action, involvement, duty and discipline should be the guiding principles of one's life. These principles were practical and easy to follow. So he decided to start Tolstoy Farm, a community of about eighty people comprising men, women and children practising different religions, speaking different languages, living and working together and sharing love and respect for each other. During the time they spent there, they were subjected to training in self-discipline and self-reliance, which in turn assisted their moral and spiritual growth.

Tolstoy Farm was far away from the city and did not offer any of the comforts of modern industrialized civilization. People lived in close proximity to nature, and since there were a large number of fruit trees and vast open spaces, adults and children were given duties like digging, chopping wood, sowing and watering. They grew their own wheat, ground it in an iron mill and baked the bread themselves. They cooked only vegetarian food which was simple, without any condiments. It must have been difficult for some inmates to do without meat, but so highly did they regard Gandhiji, they were willing to go without it. Gandhiji participated in all these chores.

Since Gandhiji found that they would be more comfortable wearing trousers and shirts when working on the farm, he started a tailoring department to stitch these garments. One of Gandhiji's associates, Hermann Kallenbach, was sent to learn how to make sandals since they were the more practical footwear and he started a workshop producing sandals for the residents and even sold some to friends. Gandhiji too was quite proficient at this task and had made fourteen pairs of sandals by February 1911.

In spite of the rigorous and very frugal lives they led, most people who lived and grew up on Tolstoy Farm recalled those days later in life with pleasure and satisfaction that the experience had made them better human beings.

If the cooperative movement became a national movement, it could bring about revolutionary changes in the social and economic structure of national life, Gandhiji said. It would ensure dignity for the poorest farmer, respect for anyone who provided a service no matter how lowly, tolerance of people of all faiths and a more equal distribution of wealth.

These principles do not apply only to the political or economic spheres, nor are they relevant only to rural areas, to farmers, craftsmen, skilled and semi-skilled labourers, or what is called the unorganized sector. Today many of us live in communities or housing societies, in multi-storeyed apartment blocks. We share our space with people of diverse backgrounds, cultures and professions. It is important for us to cultivate the spirit of cooperation, of consideration for each other, if we are to live in harmony and peace with each other.

I hold that self-government is . . . only a means to good government. And true democracy is what promotes the welfare of the people. The test of good government lies in the largest good of the people with the minimum of control . . . In my view a system that admits of poverty and unemployment is not fit to survive even for a day.

Collected Works of Mahatma Gandhi, vol. 90
(Publications Division, Govt. of India, 1960, p. 325)

We stand today in danger of forgetting how to use our hands. To forget how to dig the earth and tend the soil is to forget ourselves. To think that your occupation of the Ministerial chair will be vindicated if you serve the cities only would be to forget that India really resides in her 7,00,000 village units. What would it profit a man if he gained the world but lost his soul in the bargain?

Harijan, 25 August 1946

[Gandhiji had the vision of a Samagra Gramseva] in which the Gramsevak must know everybody living in the village and render them such service as he can . . . He will show them the way of helping themselves and procure for them such help and materials as they require. This is my conception of a Samagra Gramaseva . . . After all the man who runs an oil mill is a ghanchi. He has money but his strength does not lie in his money. Real strength lies in knowledge. True knowledge gives a moral standing and moral strength.

Harijan, 17 March 1946

I would say that, if the village perishes, India will perish too. India will be no more India. Her own mission in the world will get lost. The revival of the village is possible only when it is no more exploited. Industrialization on a mass scale will necessarily lead to a passive or active exploitation of the villagers as the problems of competition and marketing come in.

Therefore, we have to concentrate on the village being self-contained, manufacturing mainly for use. Provided this character of the village industry is maintained, there would be no objection to villagers using even the modern machines and tools that they can make and can afford to use. Only, they should not be used as a means of exploitation of others.

Harijan, 29 August 1936

We have to make a choice between India of the villages that are as ancient as herself and India of the cities which are a creation of foreign domination. Today the cities dominate and drain the villages so that they are crumbling to ruin. My Khadi mentality tells me that cities must subserve villages when that domination goes. Exploiting of villages is itself organized violence; we will have to give the villages their proper place.

Harijan, 20 January 1940

It is only when the cities realize the duty of making an adequate return to the villages for the strength and sustenance which they derive from them, instead of selfishly exploiting them, that a healthy and moral relationship between the two will spring up. And if the city children are to play their part in this great and noble work of social reconstruction, the vocations through which they are to receive their education ought to be directly related to the requirements of the villages.

Harijan, 19 October 1937

Independence must begin at the bottom. Thus, every village will be a republic or Panchayat having full powers. It follows therefore, that every village has to be selfsustained and capable of managing its affairs even

to the extent of defending itself against the whole world
. . . ultimately it is the individual who is the unit. This
does not exclude dependence on and willing help from
neighbours or from the world. It will be free and voluntary
play of mutual forces. Such a society is necessarily
highly cultured, in which every man and woman knows
what he or she wants, and what is more, knows that no
one should want anything that others cannot have with
equal labour. This society must naturally be based on
Truth and Non-violence which in my opinion, are not
possible without a living belief in God . . .

Harijan, 1 July 1947

It is the function of the Panchayats to revive honesty
and industry . . . It is the function of the Panchayats
to teach the villagers to avoid disputes, if they have to
settle them. This will ensure speedy justice without any
expenditure. You will need neither the police nor the
military.

Harijan, 4 January 1948

The Real India lies in the 7,00,000 villages. If Indian civilization is to make its full contribution to the building up of a stable world order, it is this vast mass of humanity that has . . . to be made to live again.

Harijan, 27 April 1947

You cannot build non-violence on a factory civilization, but it can be built on self-contained villages . . . Rural economy as I have conceived it, eschews exploitation altogether, and exploitation is the essence of violence. You have, therefore, to be rural-minded before you can be non-violent, and to be rural-minded you have to have faith in the spinning-wheel.

Harijan, 4 November 1939

The very first problem the village worker will solve is its sanitation. It is the most neglected of all the problems that baffle workers and that undermine physical well-being and breed disease. If the worker became a voluntary bhangi, he would begin by collecting night soil and turning it into manure and sweeping village streets. He will tell people how and where they should perform daily functions and speak to them on the value of sanitation and the great injury caused by its neglect.

Harijan, 9 January 1937

In this village of my dreams the villager will not be dull . . . he will not live like an animal in filth and darkness. Men and women will live in freedom . . . There will be no plague, no cholera and no smallpox. Everyone will have to do body labour.

Discussions with executive members of the Gandhi Seva Sangh, May 1939

No municipality can cope with insanitation and congestion by the simple process of taxation and paid services. This vital reform is possible only by wholesale and voluntary cooperation of the people both rich and poor.

Young India, 19 November 1925

TRUSTEESHIP

'The earth has enough for man's need but not enough for man's greed.'

What did Gandhiji mean by this oft-quoted remark? Was he trying to warn us about our indiscriminate exploitation of our natural resources? Yes, he was. But because his words went largely unheeded, environmental degradation has become one of the biggest worries for all of us.

The primary concern of conservationists, ecologists, environmentalists and ordinary sensitive people is to make people realize that our natural resources are limited. If we continue to misuse the land, water bodies and energy sources, future generations will find it difficult to survive.

If we think the problem doesn't really concern us, let us look at the immediate repercussions we will face — global warming, climate change, deforestation and ecological imbalance will all affect our lives. Unchecked use of natural resources will lead to serious conflicts among people. Resources belong to all inhabitants of this planet, but not all have access to them, nor has everybody benefited fairly from them. There is still grave inequality in the distribution of wealth and its attendant — power. In order to obtain what we want we will go to any lengths to get it — whether by fair means or foul.

This tendency led Gandhiji to evolve the principle of trusteeship. He was convinced that unless we simplify our lives and limit our needs, we will remain avaricious, become hoarders and grab for ourselves as much as we can, with no thought for others.

He said that it is our responsibility to look after the precious natural resources we have been given; to nurture, preserve them and give back at least in part what we take out of it. It came to us from previous generations, let us hand it over to the future in as good a condition as we got it. The principle of trusteeship, which is considering ourselves only guardians or caretakers, not owners, was the only tool for bringing about economic equality in society. Gandhiji did not believe that heavy taxation or joint ownership would get the desired result. Both these methods would lead to resentment and violence. He believed that human beings should be persuaded to show compassion, sympathy, care and love for each other. If they cultivated these qualities they would never think of their own comfort and happiness at the cost of someone else's, they would not bully or exploit another, or deny anyone their right to live with dignity and self-respect.

But trusteeship is not only about economic principles. It applies as much to human relationships. Parents are trustees of their children's lives. They are responsible for inculcating in their offspring a value system that enables them to lead an upright, moral life. It is the duty of teachers to train the minds of their pupils so that they become well-informed, rational beings, with the ability to discriminate, distinguish and debate (on issues). Owners of industry are trustees of their workers and they must ensure the welfare of their employees. Today most industrial houses and businesses are very conscious of their 'corporate social responsibility'. Even governments are trustees of the power vested in them and they owe it to the people to provide them the basic amenities for decent living and, most importantly, assure every individual an opportunity to grow, develop and flourish in whatever field of activity, as long as it is for the common good of all. Gandhiji did not believe in the greatest good of the largest number, but the greatest good of all.

A trustee has no heir but the public. In a State built on the basis of non-violence, the commission of trustees will be regulated.

Harijan, 12 April 1942

Under State-regulated trusteeship, an individual will not be free to hold or use his wealth for selfish satisfaction or in disregard of the interests of society.

Harijan, 25 October 1952

You may say that trusteeship is a legal fiction. But if people meditate over it constantly and try to act up to it, then life on earth would be governed far more by love than it is at present. Absolute trusteeship is an abstraction . . . But if we strive for it, we shall be able to go further in realizing a state of equality on earth than by any other method.

The Modern Review, 1935

Trusteeship provides a means of transforming the present capitalist order of society into an egalitarian one. It gives no quarter to capitalism, but gives the present owning class a chance of reforming itself. It is based on the faith that human nature is never beyond redemption.

Harijan, 25 October 1952

In the modern rush, the chief use we have for our rivers is to empty our gutters in them and navigate our cargo vessels, and in the process make them dirtier still. We have no time . . . to stroll down to these rivers, and in silent meditation listen to the message they murmur to us.

Young India, 23 December 1926

RELIGION, CASTE AND SECULARISM

Have you ever been asked to write which religion you belong to in a form, or even in school? In the school assembly, have you heard bits from different scriptures being read and wondered who wrote them?

Religion is generally associated with God, places of worship, rituals and ceremonies, festivals and celebrations. It is also a set of values that dictate the way we think and behave in society. In India a number of religions coexist. Sometimes people of one religion get into a confrontation with people of another religion. This leads to violence. But mostly we live together in harmony, giving each other the space to practise our beliefs. This aspect of our country, where many religions are given equal rights of practice, is called secularism, and it is something that makes most Indians proud.

Gandhiji was a profoundly religious man. He was proud to call himself a Hindu. But he also made deep studies of other religions like Christianity and Islam by reading their holy texts. He said there could not be superiority of one religion over the others. That is what secularism really means and Gandhiji wanted all of us to understand and be truly secular in our thinking. His philosophy of ahimsa emphasized the same respect for the religious faith of others as for one's own.

Gandhiji was also fully aware of the shortcomings of Hinduism as it was being practised. He saw that religion was being confused with empty ritual. Just reading the sacred texts is not enough, he said. One must understand them and live according to their teachings. It is not wise to accept traditions because they are ancient, without questioning. One must not hesitate to give up any tradition that is not consistent with morality or if it is in conflict with reason, he advised.

That is why he had no qualms about not wearing the sacred thread when he learnt that only the upper castes were allowed to wear it and Shudras were forbidden from putting it on. A religious symbol that made a distinction between man and man did not deserve to be honoured, he said. We are all God's creations, and there is God in all of us.

On the other hand, he was quick to admit that he had been wrong to shave off his tuft when he went to England to study law, for reasons of vanity, because he was embarrassed by it. So he decided to grow it again and kept it all his life.

Gandhiji was deeply saddened by the dirt and filth surrounding temples, the way nature had been defiled in holy places like Rishikesh and Haridwar. But what caused him the greatest anguish was the caste system that declared one group of people inferior to others. All his life he struggled to have the poorest, lowliest of human beings accepted into the mainstream, and to get them respectability and economic upliftment.

Despite the efforts of the government to continue Gandhiji's struggle against the caste system, people are still doing utterly inhuman jobs in India today.

In Gandhiji's ideal world, towards which we should all strive, we will share our space with another human being with love, regardless of his religion, caste, colour or profession.

Religions are different roads converging upon the same point. What does it matter that we take different roads so long as we reach the same goal?

Hind Swaraj, 1909

I believe that, if in spite of the best of intentions, one is led into committing mistakes, they do not really result in harm to the world or, for the matter of that, any individual. God always saves the world from the consequences of unintended errors of men who live in fear of Him.

Those who are likely to be misled by my example would have gone that way all the same even if they had not known of my action. For, in the final analysis, a man is guided in his conduct by his own inner promptings, though the example of others might sometimes seem to guide him.

Young India, 3 January 1929

I believe in the fundamental truth of all great religions of the world. I believe that they are all God-given, and I believe that they were necessary for the people to whom these religions were revealed. And I believe that, if only we could all of us read the scriptures of the different faiths from the standpoint of the followers of those faiths, we should find that they were at the bottom all one and were all helpful to one another.

Harijan, 16 February 1934

God is Truth, but God is many other things also. That is why I say Truth is God . . . Only remember that Truth is not one of the many qualities we name. It is the living embodiment of God, it is the only Life, and I identify Truth with the fullest life, and that is how it becomes a concrete thing, for God is His whole creation, the whole Existence, and service of all that exists — Truth — is service of God.

Harijan, 25 May, 1935

I am endeavouring to see God through service of humanity, for I know that God is neither in heaven, nor down below, but in every one.

Young India, 4 August 1927

Let me explain what I mean by religion. It is not the Hindu religion which I certainly prize above all other religions, but the religion which transcends Hinduism, which changes one's very nature, which binds one indissolubly to the truth within and which ever purifies. It is the permanent element in human nature which counts no cost too great in order to find full expression and which leaves the soul utterly restless until it has found itself, known its Maker and appreciated the true correspondence between the Maker and itself.

Young India, 12 May 1920

God has a thousand names, or rather, He is Nameless. We may worship or pray to Him by whichever name that pleases us. Some call Him Rama, some Krishna, others call Him Rahim, and yet others call Him God. All worship the same spirit, but as all foods do not agree with all, all names do not appeal to all. Each chooses the name according to his associations, and He, being the In-Dweller, All-powerful and Omniscient, knows our innermost feelings and responds to us according to our deserts.

Worship or prayer, therefore, is not to be performed with the lips, but with the heart.

Young India, 24 September 1925

My Hinduism is not sectarian. It includes all that I know to be best in Islam, Christianity, Buddhism and Zoroastrianism . . . Truth is my religion and ahimsa is the only way of its realization. I have rejected once and for all the doctrine of the sword.

Harijan, 30 April 1938

My religion is a matter solely between my Maker and myself. If I am a Hindu, I cannot cease to be one even though I may be disowned by the whole of the Hindu population. I do however suggest that non-violence is the end of all religions.

Young India, 29 May 1924

I do not believe that the State can concern itself or cope with religious education. I believe that religious education must be the sole concern of religious associations. Do not mix up religion and ethics. I believe that fundamental ethics is common to all religions. Teaching of fundamental ethics is undoubtedly a function of the State. By religion I have not in mind fundamental ethics but what goes by the name of denominationalism. We have suffered enough from State-aided religion and a State Church. A society or a group, which depends partly or wholly on State aid for the existence of its religion, does not deserve, or better still, does not have any religion worth the name.

Harijan, 23 March 1947

When the mind is completely filled with His spirit, one cannot harbour ill-will or hatred towards anyone and, reciprocally, the enemy will shed his enmity and become a friend. It is not my claim that I have succeeded in converting enemies into friends, but in numerous cases it has been my experience that, when the mind is filled with His peace, all hatred ceases. An unbroken succession of world teachers since the beginning of time have borne testimony to the same.

I claim no merit for it. I know it is entirely due to God's grace.

Harijan, 28 April 1946

Religion is a personal matter which should have no place in politics.

Harijan, 9 August 1942

There is no such thing as absolute morality for all times. But there is a relative morality which is absolute enough for imperfect mortals that we are.

Harijan, 23 December 1939

I do not share the belief that there can or will be on earth one religion. I am striving, therefore, to find a common factor and to induce mutual tolerance.

Young India, 3 January 1929

Belief in one God is the corner-stone of all religions. But I do not foresee a time when there would be only one religion on earth in practice. In theory, since there is one God, there can be only one religion. But in practice no two persons I have known have had the same identical conception of God. Therefore, there will, perhaps always be different religions answering to different temperaments and climatic conditions.

Harijan, 2 February 1934

I believe that all the great religions of the world are true more or less. I say 'more or less' because I believe that everything that the human hand touches, by reason of the very fact that human beings are imperfect, becomes imperfect. Perfection is the exclusive attribute of God and it is indescribable, untranslatable. I do believe that it is possible for every human being to become perfect even as God is perfect. It is necessary for us all to aspire after perfection, but when that blessed state is attained, it becomes indescribable, indefinable. And I therefore admit, in all humility, that even the Vedas, the Koran and the Bible are imperfect word of God and, imperfect beings that we are, swayed to and fro by a multitude of passions, it is impossible for us even to understand this word of God in its fullness.

Young India, 22 September 1927

Religions are not meant for separating men from one another, they are meant to bind them.

Harijan, 8 June 1940

Man should earnestly desire the well-being of all God's creation and pray that we may have the strength to do so. In desiring the well-being of all, he's his own welfare; he who desires only his own or his community's welfare is selfish and it can never be well with him.

Harijan, 27 October 1946

Indeed, religion should pervade every one of our actions. Here religion does not mean sectarianism. It means a belief in ordered moral government of the universe. It is no less real because it is unseen. This religion transcends Hinduism, Islam, Christianity, etc. It does not supersede them. It harmonizes them and gives them reality.

Harijan, 13 July 1940

God answers prayer in His own way, not ours. His ways are different from the ways of mortals. Hence they are inscrutable. Prayer presupposes faith. No prayer goes in vain. Prayer is like any other action. It bears fruit whether we see it or not, and the fruit of heart prayer is far more potent than action so-called.

Harijan, 29 June 1946.

By detachment I mean that you must not worry whether the desired result follows from your action or not, so long as your motive is pure, your means correct ... It means that things will come right in the end if you take care of the means and leave the rest to Him.

Harijan, 7 April 1946

[When the atom bomb was dropped on Hiroshima, Gandhiji was asked how his non-violence and Truth would fit into the new scheme of things. His answer was:]

Do I still adhere to my faith in truth and nonviolence? Has not the atom bomb exploded that faith? Not only has it not done so but it has clearly demonstrated to me that the twins constitute the mightiest force in the world. Before it (Satya and Ahimsa) the atom bomb is of no effect.

Harijan, 2 February 1946

Ahimsa is not the goal. Truth is the goal. But we have no means of realizing Truth in human relationships except through the practice of ahimsa. A steadfast pursuit of ahimsa is inevitably bound to Truth — not so violence. That is why I swear by ahimsa. Truth came naturally to me. Ahimsa I acquired after a struggle.

But ahimsa being the means, we are naturally more concerned with it in our everyday life. It is ahimsa, therefore, that our masses have to be educated in. Education in Truth follows from it as a natural end.

Harijan, 23 June 1946

Nobody in this world knows absolute Truth. This is God's attribute alone. Relative Truth is all we know. Therefore, we can only follow the Truth as we see it. Such pursuit of Truth cannot lead anyone astray.

Harijan, 2 June 1946

I call that great power not by the name of Allah, not by the name of Khuda or God, but by the name of Truth. For me Truth is God and Truth overrides all our plans. The whole truth is only embodied within the heart of that Great power — Truth. I was taught from my early days to regard Truth as un-approachable — something that you cannot reach. A great Englishman taught me to believe that God is unknowable. He is knowable, but knowable only to the extent that our limited intellect allows.

Harijan, 20 April 1947

Every religion has its full and equal place. We are all leaves of a majestic tree whose trunk cannot be shaken off its roots which are deep down in the bowels of the earth. The mightiest wind cannot move it.

Harijan, 28 July 1946

The State is bound to be wholly secular . . . All subjects will thus be equal in the eye of the law. But every single individual will be free to pursue a religion without let or hindrance so long as it does not transgress the common law.

Harijan, 31 August 1947

The minorities must be made to realize that they are as much valued citizens of the State they live in as the majority of the State.

Harijan, 7 September 1947

In battling against untouchability and in dedicating myself to that battle, I have no less an ambition than to see a complete regeneration of humanity. It may be a mere dream, as unreal as the silver in the sea-shell. It is not so to me while the dream lasts, and in the words of Romain Rolland, 'Victory lies not in realization of the goal, but in a relentless pursuit after it.'

Harijan, 25 March 1933

Free India will be no Hindu raj, it will be Indian raj, based not on the majority of any religious sect or community but on the representatives of the whole people without distinction of religion.

Harijan, 9 August 1942

I swear by my religion. I will die for it. But the State has nothing to do with it. The State would look after your secular welfare, health, communications, foreign relations, currency and so on, but not your or my religion. That is everybody's personal concern.

Harijan, 22 September 1946

My patriotism is not an exclusive thing. It is all-embracing and I should reject that patriotism which sought to mount upon the distress of exploitation of other nationalities. The conception of my patriotism is nothing if it is not always, in every case without exception, consistent with the broadest good of humanity at large. Not only that, but my religion and my patriotism, derived from my religion, embrace all life. I want to realize brotherhood or identity not merely with the beings called human, but . . . all life in whatever form it appears must be essentially one.

Young India, 18 June 1925